A LAMP
FOR MY FEET
AND A
LIGHT
FOR MY PATH

for catholic
TEENS

A
LAMP
FOR MY FEET
AND A
LIGHT
FOR MY PATH

by Nancy Humes

EMMAUS
ROAD
PUBLISHING

Steubenville, Ohio
A Division of Catholics United for the Faith

Emmaus Road Publishing
827 North Fourth Street
Steubenville, OH 43952

Library of Congress Control Number: 2006939662
ISBN: 978-1-931018-43-2

Cover design and layout by
Beth Hart

Table of Contents . . . . *v*

Introduction . . . . *vii*

LESSON ONE
Who Do You Say That I Am? *1*

LESSON TWO
The Amazing Character of God *5*

LESSON THREE
Lord, Teach Us to Pray *9*

LESSON FOUR
The Fruits of the Holy Spirit *13*

LESSON FIVE
The Gifts of the Holy Spirit *17*

LESSON SIX
Jesus is Born—The First Coming *21*

LESSON SEVEN
Jesus is Coming Again—Be Ready *25*

LESSON EIGHT
The Reality of Heaven and Hell *29*

LESSON NINE
Satan and Spiritual Warfare. *33*

LESSON TEN
How God Defines Love 37

LESSON ELEVEN
God's Gift of Sexuality 41

LESSON TWELVE
God's Command to Obey 45

LESSON THIRTEEN
God's Order for the Family 49

LESSON FOURTEEN
Your Relationship With Your Parents 53

LESSON FIFTEEN
Right to Choose vs. Right to Life 57

LESSON SIXTEEN
Contentment 61

LESSON SEVENTEEN
The Real Meaning of Good Self-Esteem 65

LESSON EIGHTEEN
Controlling the Tongue 69

LESSON NINETEEN
Dealing With Disappointment 73

LESSON TWENTY
Unforgivingness—Recipe for Bitterness 77

INTRODUCTION

God wants everyone to come to know and love Him. The Scriptures reveal a great deal about Our Lord—His plan for our salvation, details about His character, and what He expects of those who wish to follow Him. In other words, God's Word is a glimpse into the mind of our Creator!

This Bible study was written with consideration for the problems and challenges young people face today. Because the Bible is inspired by God, and therefore timeless, it is as relevant today as the day it was written, and the principles apply to our modern age.

Hopefully, after completing this study, the students will not only be more familiar with the Scriptures and will have learned the importance of applying them to their daily lives, but will also see the need to begin a closer, more personal walk with the One who gave His life that we might have the hope of eternal life!

WHO DO YOU
SAY THAT I AM?

How do you fall in Love w/someone Refer back added

In order to love someone, we must first get to know him or her. The Scriptures tell us who God is and how He thinks. Jesus wants to be the most important person in your life. It is natural to want to spend time with those we love. The following study will help you determine where God fits in your life.

READ

1. Who did some people think Jesus was while He was on earth? (Matthew 16: 13–14)

   _____

   _____

   _____

2. What did Peter say he believed about Jesus? (Matthew 16:16)

   _____

   _____

   _____

3. Who revealed to Peter the identity of Jesus? (Matthew 16:17)

   _____

   _____

   _____

4. To some, Jesus is no more than a historical figure. To others, He is truly "the way, the truth, and the life." Look up the following Scriptures and write what Jesus wants to be to you.

John 3:16 _____

_____

_____

John 10:11 _____

_____

_____

John 13:15 _____

_____

_____

John 14:6 _____

_____

_____

John 14:14 _____

_____

_____

John 15:5 _____

_____

_____

John 15:13–17 _____

_____

_____

5. Many times we say we love Jesus, but our actions do not reflect this. What do you think it means to give God "lip service?" (Isaiah 29:13)

_____

_____

_____

6. How can we prove our love for Jesus? (John 14:15)

_____

_____

_____

2

REFLECT

1. Write a few sentences describing your relationship with Jesus.

_____

_____

_____

2. On a scale of 1 to 10, what place does He have in your life at this time? Explain.

_____

_____

_____

RESPOND

1. Set a time aside each day for prayer. Pick a quiet place and try to make this a priority in your daily schedule.

2. Go to daily Mass whenever possible. Mass is the perfect prayer, and we should try to go beyond our Sunday obligation.

3. Try to receive the sacrament of Reconciliation once a month.

Memory Scripture
John 14:15

"If you love me, you will keep my commandments."

3

THE AMAZING
CHARACTER OF GOD

When we meditate on the Scriptures, we get a glimpse into the heart and mind of God. The Bible tells us that if we seek God, we will find Him. As you give thought to the next study, consider the awesome character of the Creator of the Universe!

READ

1. God is love: How deep is God's love for us? (Jeremiah 31:3)

2. God is supreme: What does Psalm 95:3 say about God?

3. God is all-powerful: What were the Angel Gabriel's words to Mary? (Luke 1:37)

4. God knows everything: What does Hebrews 4:13 say about God's knowledge?

5. God is wise: What did Daniel say about God's wisdom? (Daniel 2:20)

   _____

   _____

   _____

6. God is everywhere: How did King David describe God's omnipresence? (1 Kings 8:27)

   _____

   _____

   _____

7. God is unchanging: In a world where things are constantly changing, what is one thing we can count on? (Malachi 3:6)

   _____

   _____

   _____

8. God is faithful: What do we learn about God's faithfulness in Deuteronomy 7:9?

   _____

   _____

   _____

9. God is holy: When we consider holy people what must we remember? (Revelations 15:4)

   _____

   _____

   _____

10. God is just: What does God's justice come against? (Romans 1:18)

   _____

   _____

   _____

REFLECT

1. At what times do you think we are most apt to doubt God's love for us?

    _____

    _____

    _____

2. Since God spoke the universe into existence, how should this affect how we see Him?

    _____

    _____

    _____

RESPOND

1. If you have a habit of taking God's name in vain, stop today.

2. The next time you receive Communion, remember God is in your mouth!

Memory Scripture
Psalm 33:8

"Let all the earth
fear the LORD."

7

LORD, TEACH US TO PRAY

Conversation is one of the most important components of a relationship. Prayer is the vehicle we use to speak to God and He with us. Since He often speaks in a still, small voice, it is important that we listen carefully. God wants to speak to you. Will you give Him an attentive ear?

READ

1. When Jesus' disciples asked Him to teach them to pray, what was His response? (Luke 11:1–4)

_____

_____

_____

_____

2. What should we keep in mind when we are making requests of the Lord? (1 John 5:14–15)

_____

_____

_____

3. How often should we pray? (1 Thessalonians 5:17)

_____

_____

_____

4. Which of your activities can be considered a prayer? (Colossians 3:17)

_____

_____

_____

5. What do the Scriptures say are some reasons for unanswered prayer? (James 4:3, Sirach 3:5, Matthew 6: 5–7, 1 John 1:8–10)

_____

_____

_____

_____

_____

REFLECT

1. What are some ways God has answered your prayers in the way you had hoped?

_____

_____

_____

2. Have there been times when you asked God for things that you knew in your heart would not be His will for you? Explain.

_____

_____

_____

3. How do you think prayer and reading the Scriptures could help you determine God's will for your life?

_____

_____

_____

4. Tell about a time when you felt God did not answer your prayer.

_____

_____

_____

RESPOND

1. Try using the following as a guideline (ACTS) for prayer:

Adore God, praise Him.
Confess your sins to Him in prayer.

Thank God for all that He's done for you.
Supplication (requests). Remember others in prayer.

2. Pray for God's will in your life.

3. Pray for your enemies.

Memory Scripture
Luke 11:1

"Lord, teach us to pray..."

THE FRUITS
OF THE HOLY SPIRIT

*Y*ou recognize the value of a tree by the fruit it bears (see Matthew 7:17–19). The fruit of a person's spiritual life is manifested by his or her actions.

It is the Holy Sprit, working in the person's life that makes this possible. When we were baptized, we received the Holy Spirit for the first time and our parents claimed us for Christ and the Church. When we receive the sacrament of Confirmation, the sacrament completes the baptismal grace. We then have a greater obligation to spread the faith and defend it against attack (CCC 1285).

READ

1. Who is the Holy Spirit? (Matthew 28:19)

   _____
   _____
   _____

2. What is one of the functions of the Holy Spirit? (John 14:26)

   _____
   _____
   _____

3. Jesus said people would know Christians by their fruit. What did He mean? (Matthew 7:16)

   _____
   _____
   _____

4. Name the fruits of the Holy Spirit. (Galatians 5:22–23)

   _____

   _____

   _____

5. Read the parable of the fig tree (Luke 13:6–9). What do you think the story is telling Christians?

   _____

   _____

   _____

   _____

REFLECT

1. Can people tell by your actions, speech, and the way you dress that you belong to Jesus?

   _____

   _____

   _____

2. List some good fruits you are displaying at this time.

   _____

   _____

   _____

3. Is there any bad fruit you think the Lord might want to prune away from your character? Write down one thing you think He might want to change.

   _____

   _____

   _____

RESPOND

1. Pray this prayer every day:

   Holy Spirit, enlighten my mind that I might seek, know, and obey the teachings of the Catholic Church. Help me to be steadfast in living out my baptismal promise to avoid what is evil and seek what is holy, and give me the gift of courage, that I might boldly share my faith with others to further the Kingdom of God.

   Amen.

2. Confess your serious faults in Reconciliation.

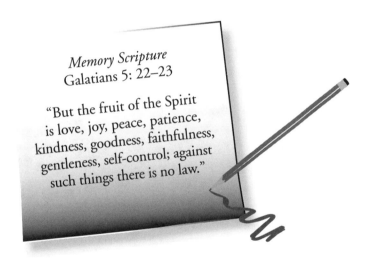

Memory Scripture
Galatians 5: 22–23

"But the fruit of the Spirit is love, joy, peace, patience, kindness, goodness, faithfulness, gentleness, self-control; against such things there is no law."

THE GIFTS
OF THE HOLY SPIRIT
Wisdom, Understanding, Knowledge, Courage,
Judgment, Piety, Fear of the Lord

*A*s members of the Body of Christ, we are given certain gifts that enable us to become fruitful Christians. If someone gave you a gift, wouldn't you open it immediately? The spiritual gifts we receive from the Holy Spirit must also be unwrapped and used. The following study will help you understand the importance of the Gifts of the Holy Spirit and also make you more aware of the need for them in your daily life.

READ

1. If we lack wisdom, what must we do? (James 1:5)

   _____
   _____
   _____

2. What do wise people do? (Proverbs 10:14)

   _____
   _____
   _____

3. What did King Solomon ask of God? (1 Kings 3:9)

   _____
   _____
   _____

4. What was Jesus' warning to us as Christians? (John 16:33)

5. Why do we need the Gift of Judgment? (Ephesians 5:17)

6. What does God demand of His children? (1 Peter 1:14–16)

7. What is the advantage of having reverence or fear of the Lord? (Proverbs 19:23)

REFLECT

1. After studying the above Scriptures, what do you think is the greatest reason for a Christian to have the Gifts of the Holy Spirit?

2. Which of the Gifts of the Holy Spirit would you most desire? Why?

3. How important is good judgment in the life of a teenager today? Explain your answer.

RESPOND

1. Pray that the Holy Spirit will show you the importance of His gifts in your life.

2. Remember that a Christian who tries to go through life without the power of the Holy Spirit is like buying a new car and pushing it instead of filling it up with gas!

3. When it comes to courage, remember that the Apostles were afraid before Pentecost and bold after they were filled by the Holy Spirit.

Memorize the
Gifts of the Holy Spirit

Wisdom,
Understanding,
Knowledge, Courage,
Judgment, Piety,
Fear of the Lord

JESUS IS BORN—
THE FIRST COMING

*T*he miracle of the Incarnation occurred when God took on the flesh of man. It is the most remarkable event to have ever taken place. Our Lady said "yes" to God even through she didn't fully understand all of the details. Mary and Joseph trusted God with their lives. As you study this lesson, try to think of some ways to make Christmas "real" in your heart.

READ

1. What are three reasons why Mary would have been confused and even fearful upon hearing the angel's news that she would be the mother of Jesus? (Luke 1: 29, Matthew 1:18–19, Deuteronomy 22:23–24)

   _____

   _____

   _____

   _____

2. What was Mary's response to the angel of the Lord, in spite of her confusion? (Luke 1:38)

   _____

   _____

   _____

3. What are some details in Scripture that indicate that Joseph and Mary were poor? (Leviticus 12:8, Luke 2:24, Luke 2:7)

   _____

   _____

   _____

4. What do the Scriptures say about the act of giving? (Acts 20:35)

5. What are some ways we can prepare spiritually for Christmas? (1 John 1:9, Matthew 5:42, Colossians 4:2)

6. What was the primary purpose for Jesus, who is God, to become man? (John 3:16, 1 Thessalonians 5:9–10)

REFLECT

1. Why do you think Our Lady was able to say "yes" to God, even though she was afraid?

2. In what ways do you think Christmas has become commercialized? Why is this contrary to the real meaning of Christmas?

3. What is the greatest gift you could give your family?

RESPOND

1. Go to Confession during advent.

2. Help your parents with shopping, cleaning, wrapping presents, or other tasks.

3. Give a portion of your allowance to the poor.

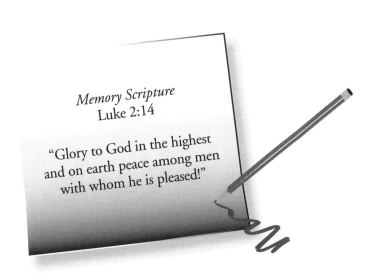

Memory Scripture
Luke 2:14

"Glory to God in the highest and on earth peace among men with whom he is pleased!"

JESUS IS COMING AGAIN— BE READY!

*T*hose who love God should have no fear of the Second Coming. The Church teaches that we do not know when or how Jesus will come again, only that He will. The Scriptures warn us to be prepared. God is merciful and forgiving and wants all people to be saved. It is important to live a holy life, but when we sin, we know that the sacrament of Reconciliation restores our union with God.

READ

1. When will Jesus come again? (Matthew 24:36–44)

2. Will we have warnings so we can be ready? (Mark 13:1–37)

3. What advice does Paul give us in 2 Timothy 4:1–5?

_____
_____

4. Jesus came as a helpless baby the first time. How will He come the second time? (Revelations 19:11–16)

_____
_____
_____
_____
_____

5. How are we to help prepare the world for the Second Coming? (Matthew 28: 19–20)

_____
_____
_____

REFLECT

1. In what ways are you the hands, feet, and mouth of Jesus?

_____
_____
_____

2. What are some things you could be doing to prepare your own soul for judgment?

_____
_____
_____

3. In what state is your soul at this time?

_____
_____
_____

RESPOND

1. Start a Bible study or prayer group at school.

2. Ask the Holy Spirit for opportunities to share your faith this week.

3. Resolve to live every day as if it were your last.

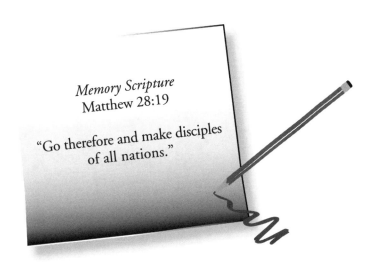

Memory Scripture
Matthew 28:19

"Go therefore and make disciples
of all nations."

THE REALITY
OF HEAVEN AND HELL

*A*s a young person, it is natural to assume that there is much time to think about eternity. However, no one knows when he will die. Think of being prepared as an investment. Your parents plan for retirement because they know they will one day grow old. The same could be said about death. We know we will one day die. The good news is that we have the opportunity to choose where we will spend eternity.

READ

1. What are some things the Scriptures tell us about Heaven? (John 14:2–3, Luke 10:20, Luke 16:22–26, 1 Corinthians 2:9)

   _____

   _____

   _____

   _____

2. What do the Scriptures say we must do in order to reach Heaven? (Matthew 7:21, Deuteronomy 6:5, John 15:12)

   _____

   _____

   _____

3. What does God tell us in His Word about Hell? (Matthew 13:41–42, Mark 9:43–44)

   _____

   _____

   _____

4. Read Luke 16:19–31. Why did the rich man go to Hell?

_____

_____

_____

REFLECT

1. Do you think many people fail to think about where they will spend eternity? Explain your answer.

_____

_____

_____

2. Many people feel frustrated about trying to live a holy life in our modern world. What are your thoughts on this problem?

_____

_____

_____

3. "Quo Vadis?" (Where are you going?) Do you have confidence about reaching Heaven? Why or why not?

_____

_____

_____

RESPOND

1. Make a good examination of conscience and go to confession, and decide to get rid of one bad habit this school year. Do something positive to take the place of the bad habit.

2. Ask the Holy Spirit to give you a reverence for God's justice and an understanding of His love and mercy.

3. Ask God for an opportunity to share your faith with someone who you know may be searching for Him.

Memory Scripture
Matthew 7:13–14

"Enter by the narrow gate; for the gate is wide and the way is easy, that leads to destruction, and those who enter by it are many. For the gate is narrow and the way is hard, that leads to life, and those who find it are few."

SATAN AND SPIRITUAL WARFARE

*T*he Scriptures tell us that Satan is our enemy. We are no match for him, but God is more powerful. Our Lord provides protection for us against Satan's tactics. The Church teaches that we must avoid the occasions of sin. This means we must be careful not to put ourselves in compromising situations. We must use our will and our Catholic training to make wise decisions in regard to friends, activities, and entertainment.

READ

1. Is Satan real or imaginary? (John 8:43–44)

   _____
   _____
   _____

2. Who is our enemy? (1 Peter 5:8)

   _____
   _____
   _____

3. Is Satan more powerful than God? (1 John 4:1–6)

   _____
   _____
   _____
   _____

4. What are our weapons against Satan? (Ephesians 6:13–18)

   _____
   _____

5. Why should we guard against activities and/or entertainment that have to do with Satan or the occult? (1 Timothy 4:1 and Deuteronomy 18:10–14)

6. What are we to allow into our minds? (Philippians 4:8 and Psalm 101:3)

REFLECT

1. Think about your entertainment. Do you think you may be compromising your morals?

2. Do you think Satan is influencing people today and that he is having an effect on society? Why or why not?

3. Do you think most young people are aware that Satan wants to influence their thinking? Explain.

RESPOND

1. Ask the Holy Spirit to show you where Satan may be influencing your thinking in regard to truthfulness, purity of mind, obedience, kindness, etc.

2. Receive the Eucharist often, pray regularly, and go to Confession often. These are great protections against the devil.

3. Pray this prayer every day:

> St. Michael the Archangel, defend us in battle.
> Be our defense against the wickedness and snares of the Devil.
> May God rebuke him, we humbly pray, and do thou,
> O Prince of the heavenly hosts, by the power of God,
> thrust into hell Satan, and all the evil spirits,
> who prowl about the world
> seeking the ruin of souls.
> *Amen.*

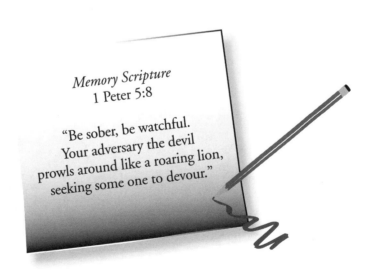

Memory Scripture
1 Peter 5:8

"Be sober, be watchful. Your adversary the devil prowls around like a roaring lion, seeking some one to devour."

HOW GOD
DEFINES LOVE

Genuine love is sacrificial. In other words, if we are concerned about the feelings and needs of the one we love, we would never ask him to do something that would cause him harm. God loves mankind perfectly. When we put God first and love as He loves, we become capable of loving more perfectly.

READ

1. Write out 1 Corinthians 13:4–8

    _____

    _____

    _____

    _____

2. How will people know that we are Christians? (John 13:35)

    _____

    _____

    _____

3. How did Jesus prove His love for us? (John 3:16)

    _____

    _____

    _____

4. How can we prove our love for Jesus? (John 14:15)

    _____

    _____

    _____

5. What should be our attitude toward those we love? (Philippians 2:3–4)

    _____

    _____

    _____

REFLECT

1. Give an example of how a person can "love" unselfishly.

    _____

    _____

    _____

2. Describe a situation when getting your own way took priority over what was best for someone else.

    _____

    _____

    _____

3. How would you define "tough love?"

    _____

    _____

    _____

RESPOND

1. This week, go out of your way to do kindnesses for those around you.

2. Remember to never ask another person to compromise his or her values.

3. Write a note or give a small gift to someone to express your love for them.

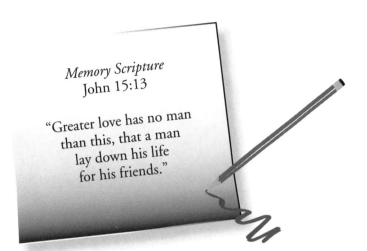

Memory Scripture
John 15:13

"Greater love has no man
than this, that a man
lay down his life
for his friends."

GOD'S GIFT
OF SEXUALITY

God created man in His image. He knows what is best for us and also what is harmful. God created sex for marriage because when two people experience this beautiful gift from God, they become one flesh. When people misuse God's gift of sexuality, they not only sin against God and themselves but also against the other person.

READ

1. In 1 Corinthians 3:16–17, what does God tell us about our bodies?

   _____

   _____

   _____

2. What do the Scriptures say about the temptations we face in life? (1 Corinthians 10:13)

   _____

   _____

   _____

3. How does God explain the difference between sins of immorality and other sins? (1 Corinthians 6:18–20)

   _____

   _____

   _____

4. How do you think applying Philippians 2:3–4 would affect your dating relationships?

_____
_____
_____

5. What does God ask of young people in 2 Timothy 2:22?

_____
_____
_____

6. What was God's perfect plan for human sexuality? (Genesis 2:24)

_____
_____
_____

7. What did Jesus say to the woman in John 8:11?

_____
_____
_____

8. In 1 John 1:9, what does God tell us about confessing any sin?

_____
_____
_____

REFLECT

1. What are several qualities that you feel are necessary for a loving relationship?

_____
_____
_____

2. What are come negative consequences that may result from misusing God's gift of sexuality?

_____
_____
_____

3. Do you think it's possible to love someone you have just recently met? Explain your answer.

_____

_____

_____

RESPOND

1. Decide today to remain pure until marriage.

2. Pray for your future spouse that God will give that person the grace to abstain from pre-marital sex.

3. Ask the Holy Spirit for grace and discernment in choosing your vocation, whether single, married, or religious.

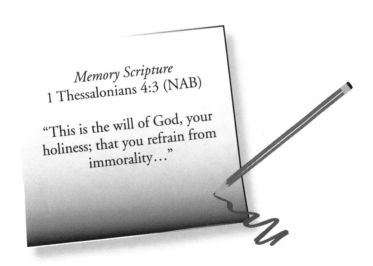

Memory Scripture
1 Thessalonians 4:3 (NAB)

"This is the will of God, your holiness; that you refrain from immorality…"

GOD'S COMMAND TO OBEY

G od's protection lies in our obedience to Him. Some may think that if we obey God, the exciting things in life will somehow pass us by. The opposite is true! When we step out from under God's protection, we open ourselves up to numerous dangers.

READ

1. What was God's warning to Adam? (Genesis 2:16–17)

_____
_____
_____

2. What did God ask of Abraham? (Genesis 22:1–14)

_____
_____
_____
_____
_____

3. Describe Jonah's response to God. (Jonah 1:1–17, Jonah 2:1–2 and 10, Jonah 3:1–3)

_____
_____
_____
_____
_____

4. When we disobey and get caught, what is a common human reaction? (Genesis 3:12–13)

_____

_____

_____

5. What do the Scriptures say about consequences to poor decision-making? (Galatians 6:7)

_____

_____

_____

REFLECT

1. Think of a time when you were disobedient. Was there a lack of peace in your heart and mind? Explain.

_____

_____

_____

2. Would God ask you to obey if it were impossible? Why or why not?

_____

_____

_____

3. Why should being obedient be considered an act of courage?

_____

_____

_____

4. Do you think you can find your own identity as a teenager without rebelling against authority? Explain your answer.

_____

_____

_____

RESPOND

1. Think of one school policy that you have not obeyed and begin today to comply to it (dress code infraction, being late to class, late assignments, etc.).

2. When someone in authority makes a request of you, do it right away. Remember that delayed obedience is disobedience.

3. Ask the Holy Spirit to show you how your disobedience is influencing and affecting other people.

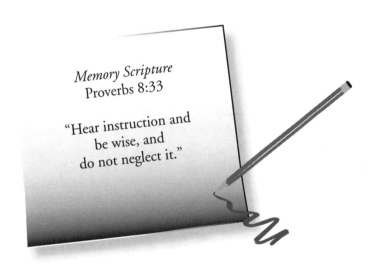

Memory Scripture
Proverbs 8:33

"Hear instruction and
be wise, and
do not neglect it."

GOD'S ORDER
FOR THE FAMILY

One need only look at nature to see that order is important to God. As a child of God, each person plays an important role in family life. It is important for you, as a young person, to realize that you have much to contribute to your family in order to make it more complete.

READ

1. How does God see men and women? (Galatians 3:26–28)

_____

_____

_____

2. Who did God place as head of the family? (Ephesians 5:23)

_____

_____

_____

3. How does God want men to love their wives? (Ephesians 5:25)

_____

_____

_____

4. What is God's command to parents? (Proverbs 22:6)

_____

_____

_____

5. What is the responsibility of children toward their parents? (Exodus 20:12 and Ephesians 6:1)

    _____

    _____

    _____

6. What does God warn parents about in Ephesians 6:4?

    _____

    _____

    _____

REFLECT

1. Read Proverbs 31:10–31 and describe, in your own words, this woman.

    _____

    _____

    _____

2. Many young people feel distanced from their parents during their teen years. What do you think are some reasons for this?

    _____

    _____

    _____

3. What are some things you could do to improve your relationship with your parents and siblings?

    _____

    _____

    _____

4. In what ways do you find it difficult to honor your Mom and Dad?

    _____

    _____

    _____

RESPOND

1. Pray each day that God will protect and bless your family.

2. Decide to do what your parents ask the first time they ask.

3. Make a resolution to keep your room clean and pick up after yourself.

Memory Scripture
Proverbs 6:20

"My son, keep your father's commandment, and forsake not your mother's teaching."

YOUR RELATIONSHIP WITH YOUR PARENTS

*T*he Fourth Commandment tells us that we must honor our parents. We do not honor them because they are perfect but because God tells us to do so. Since all humans are fallible, no person is perfect—whether parent or child. If you think of your parents as people with feelings and needs and ask what you can give rather than what you can receive, your relationship with them will improve in ways you cannot imagine.

READ

1. What does the Fourth Commandment require of you? (Exodus 20:12)

   _____
   _____
   _____

2. Even though Jesus was God, what do the Scriptures say about His relationship with His earthly parents? (Luke 2:51)

   _____
   _____
   _____

3. Do you think you can expect God to bless you if you are being consistently disobedient to your parents? (2 Timothy 3:1–5)

   _____
   _____
   _____
   _____

4. Are there times when it is acceptable to disobey your parents? (Acts 5:29)

    _____

    _____

    _____

5. What are some benefits of honoring and obeying your parents? (Sirach 3:1–15)

    _____

    _____

    _____

    _____

    _____

REFLECT

1. What actions could you change to improve your relationship with your parents?

    _____

    _____

    _____

2. Are there times when you try to irritate your parents? Have you considered what your motivation might be?

    _____

    _____

    _____

3. In your family, do you feel you're doing your part to help out at home? Explain.

    _____

    _____

    _____

RESPOND

1. When you disagree with your parents, pray before you speak.

2. Try to see things from their point of view.

3. Pray for your parents every day.

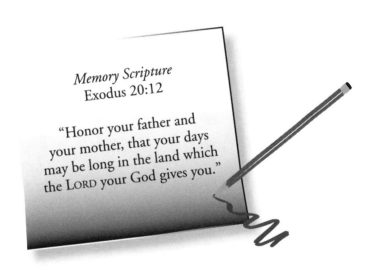

Memory Scripture
Exodus 20:12

"Honor your father and your mother, that your days may be long in the land which the LORD your God gives you."

RIGHT TO CHOOSE
VS. RIGHT TO LIFE

Since life is a gift from God, He is the only one who can give or take it away. God has a plan for every person, no matter how young or how old. God's ways are not man's ways. We cannot always trust our emotions, so we must rely on the teachings of the Church in matters of faith and morals. We must remember that the Holy Spirit guides her.

READ

1. What do the Scriptures say about the unborn? (Psalm 139:13–16, Luke 1:41)

   _____
   _____
   _____

2. Read in Isaiah 55: 8–9 about God's thinking compared to man's thinking.

   _____
   _____
   _____

3. Often, people are convinced a decision is right until they experience the consequences of their decision. What does God's Word say about this problem? (Proverbs 14:12)

   _____
   _____
   _____

4. Why must we turn to God's wisdom in difficult situations? (Proverbs 3:5–6 and Jeremiah 33:3)

_____

_____

_____

5. What are some other considerations in decision-making? (Philippians 2:3–4)

_____

_____

_____

REFLECT

1. How would you advise a friend considering an abortion?

_____

_____

_____

2. Why do many young people keep their parents out of their decision-making when they are in trouble?

_____

_____

_____

3. When should you refer a friend to a priest or another adult?

_____

_____

_____

RESPOND

1. Consider getting involved in, or starting, a pro-life group at school.

2. Pray that mothers who have aborted their children will become reconciled with God.

3. Pray that abortionists will have a change of heart.

4. Pray every day for the end to abortion.

Memory Scripture
Psalm 139:13

"For thou didst form my inward parts, thou didst knit me together in my mother's womb."

CONTENTMENT

We must always try to be all that God has called us to be. Some people confuse a person who is content with one who is dull or lacks ambition. Those who are content work hard to attain their dreams and goals but do not long for that which does not belong to them. We should seek contentment because with it comes peace of mind.

READ

1. Many people think they would be happy if their circumstances were different. What does the Bible say? (Philippians 4:11–12)

   _____

   _____

   _____

2. What did Jesus say about material wealth? (Matthew 6:19–24)

   _____

   _____

   _____

   _____

3. What do the Scriptures say about enjoying what the world has to offer? (Ecclesiastes 5:18)

   _____

   _____

   _____

4. Read Luke 16:19–31. What was the rich man's sin?

_____

_____

_____

_____

_____

5. What are the two things with which the Scriptures say we should be content? (1 Timothy 6:8)

_____

_____

_____

REFLECT

1. Do you think there is anything in the world that would make you completely happy? Explain your answer.

_____

_____

_____

2. Think of a time when you achieved a certain goal and felt somewhat letdown afterwards. Discuss.

_____

_____

_____

3. Jesus said, "Where your treasure is, there is your heart" (Matthew 6:21). What do you think He meant by this statement?

_____

_____

_____

4. What do you think the difference is between contentment and complacency?

_____

_____

_____

RESPOND

1. Ask God to help you be content with what your parents can provide.

2. God does not make junk. You have the features, body, and intellect that God planned for you. He has a marvelous plan for your life. Be glad you're you.

3. Decide not to complain for one whole day!

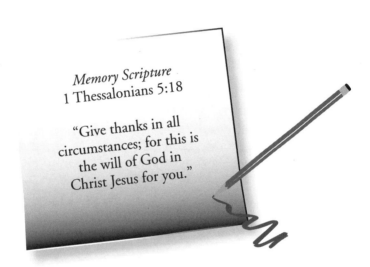

Memory Scripture
1 Thessalonians 5:18

"Give thanks in all circumstances; for this is the will of God in Christ Jesus for you."

THE REAL MEANING OF GOOD SELF-ESTEEM

*T*here are those who think that in order for people to feel good about themselves, they must receive constant compliments and encouragement. As believers, we know that if we do what is right, whether or not it is easy or popular, we will be confident and peaceful people.

READ

1. After reading 1 Samuel 16:7, describe how God sees you.

   _____

   _____

   _____

2. How precious are you to God? (Isaiah 49: 15–16)

   _____

   _____

   _____

3. What does Luke 12:7 say about how unique you are to God?

   _____

   _____

   _____

4. When God disciplines us, what should we keep in mind? (Hebrews 12:6)

   _____

   _____

   _____

5. What is the ultimate proof of how important you are to God (John 3:16)? (Put your own name in place of the pronouns in this Scripture. For example, "For God so loved Linda ...")

_____

_____

_____

REFLECT

1. List some good qualities with which God has blessed you.

_____

_____

_____

2. How do you think most people evaluate their worth?

_____

_____

_____

3. What do you think people like most about you?

_____

_____

_____

4. If you could change one thing about yourself, what would it be?

_____

_____

_____

RESPOND

1. Think about how you can use the gifts and abilities that God has given you so as to glorify Him this week.

2. When you are dissatisfied with yourself (physically, mentally, and emotionally) you are telling God that He made a mistake. Read Psalm 139:14 and meditate on your worth in God's eyes.

3. If you are unsure of your talents, ask the Holy Spirit to reveal them to you through circumstances and other people.

Memory Scripture
Psalm 139:14

"I praise thee for thou art fearful and wonderful. Wonderful are thy works! Thou knowest me right well."

CONTROLLING THE TONGUE

*T*he expression "think before you speak" is a wise saying! We must always remember that we cannot take back our words. If we had to choose between two extremes, it would be better to say too little than too much.

READ

1. What does God say about our thoughts and words in Psalm 19:15?

   _____

   _____

   _____

2. What is one of the advantages of being careful about what we say? (Proverbs 21:23)

   _____

   _____

   _____

3. To what does the Book of James compare the tongue? (James 3:3–5)

   _____

   _____

   _____

4. In James 1:19, God tells us to be _____ to hear, _____ to speak and _____ to become angry.

5. What does the Bible say about lying? (Proverbs 19: 5, 9)

   _____

   _____

   _____

6. Why should we not repeat gossip? (Proverbs 16:28)

   _____

   _____

   _____

REFLECT

1. In the last twenty-four hours, have there been times when you have spoken when you should have been quiet? Have there been times when you should have spoken up but chose not to? Describe.

   _____

   _____

   _____

2. What are some reasons, in your opinion, why people speak before they think?

   _____

   _____

   _____

3. Most people believe that lying is wrong. Why do you think so many people lie?

   _____

   _____

   _____

RESPOND

1. This week, if you have an occasion to lie or tell a half-truth, pray before you speak.

2. Decide to be quiet if you can't say something positive or kind.

3. Remember that the gossip you repeat can never be taken back.

70

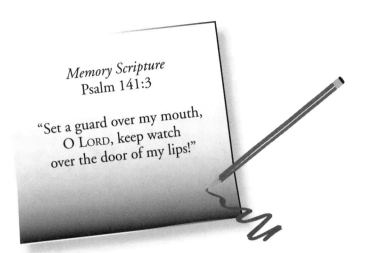

Memory Scripture
Psalm 141:3

"Set a guard over my mouth,
O LORD, keep watch
over the door of my lips!"

DEALING WITH DISAPPOINTMENT

*L*ife is often difficult but Jesus promises that He will be with us through the storms of life. We must remember that adversity produces good and strong characters. We can say with courage and confidence that God causes everything to turn out for good.

READ

1. Describe, in your own words, the meaning of John 16:33.

    _____
    _____
    _____

2. Paul asked God to remove a difficulty from his life. What was God's response? (2 Corinthians 12:7–10)

    _____
    _____
    _____

3. When Jesus was in the Garden of Gethsemane, He was suffering terribly. What did He say to His Heavenly Father (Matthew 26:39)?

    _____
    _____
    _____

4. What do the following Scriptures say about suffering?

    _____
    _____
    _____

2 Corinthians 7:10 _____

_____

_____

Romans 8:28 _____

_____

_____

1 Corinthians 10:13 _____

_____

_____

Ecclesiastes 7:14 _____

_____

_____

Philippians 1:29 _____

_____

_____

Hebrews 12:11 _____

_____

_____

James 1:2–3 _____

_____

_____

REFLECT

1. What are some common ways that people respond when they don't get their way?

_____

_____

_____

2. What would you say to someone who complains that life isn't fair?

_____

_____

_____

3. What are some things you have learned from your disappointments?

_____

_____

_____

RESPOND

1. Stop wishing it were yesterday or tomorrow. Enjoy today!

2. Follow through on commitments this week so that you won't be a source of disappointment to others.

3. Pray for the grace to offer up the pain and sacrifices of your life for Jesus' sake.

Memory Scripture
Philippians 2:14

"Do all things without grumbling or questioning…"

UNFORGIVINGNESS— RECIPE FOR BITTERNESS

*T*hose who carry grudges look at the mistakes and failures of others and ignore their own faults. If we are constantly aware of our own sinfulness and weakness, we will be less apt to dwell on the flaws of others.

READ

1. How many times should we forgive those who have hurt us? (Matthew 18:21–22)

   _____

   _____

   _____

2. What does Jesus say will happen if we don't forgive others? (Matthew 6:15)

   _____

   _____

   _____

3. How are we to see the faults of others? (Matthew 7:3–5)

   _____

   _____

   _____

4. What do the Scriptures say in regard to how we treat those who are unkind toward us? (Luke 6:32–35)

   _____

   _____

   _____

5. What did Jesus say about those who were crucifying Him? (Luke 23:34)

_____

_____

_____

6. What does Jesus tell us in Matthew 5:44?

_____

_____

_____

REFLECT

1. Are you holding a grudge against anyone?

_____

_____

_____

2. Who do you think unforgivingness hurts the most? Explain your answer.

_____

_____

_____

3. What are some reasons people give to excuse their unforgivingness toward others?

_____

_____

_____

RESPOND

1. Confess your sins of bitterness and anger in Reconciliation.

2. Think of someone who you are angry with and be the first to begin reconciliation.

3. Remember, the only person you can change is yourself!

Memory Scripture
Matthew 6:15

"But if you do not forgive men their trespasses, neither will your Father forgive your trespasses."

Notes:

NOTES:

Notes

Notes

83

Notes

Notes

Notes

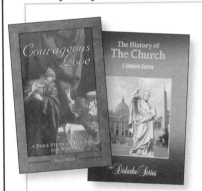